The Complete Roku Device Guide: TV, Express, Ultra, Stick, Channels, App, Account

By Bob Babson

Copyright Info:

Legal Info:

Preface

We want to take a moment to say thank you for purchasing our guide online. HiddenStuff Entertainment remains one of the top app and eBook publishers online. It is our commitment to bring you the most important information to enrich your life.

We sincerely hope that you find this guide useful and beneficial in your quest for betterment. We want to provide readers with knowledge and build their skills to perform at the highest levels within their topics of interest. This in turn contributes to a positive and more enjoyable experience. After all, it is our belief that things in life are to be enjoyed as much as they possibly can be.

If you are in need of additional support or resources in regards to this guide, please feel free to visit our webpage at Hiddenstuffentertainment.com

Contents

Getting Started

Roku's smart TV, streaming sticks, and streaming boxes all have user friendly features, but that does not mean all the useful features can be noted right away at first glance. Dig a bit more and you would discover other hidden features and tricks that are capable of making your Roku experience much better.

Keep reading for some tips:

Install your apps remotely

Trying to install your best video and music apps on a Roku can be extremely frustrating if you are doing it for the very first time. Rather than battle with your remote, employ Roku' official website Channel store for installing several apps without the normal pain and frustration. Just access your account, then search for the apps you love, and select "Add channel." Also, you could install apps with Roku application for Android and iOS.

Rearrange your channels according your preference

The first time you have your Roku, it is easy to assume that your channels are stuck in a particular order when you add them to your device. But, you can have the channel order rearranged by repositioning the channel tiles (you can do this by hovering your cursor on the channel and pressing your * button at the same time on your remote.) this will pop up a particular option menu that has "Move Channel." With your favorite channels properly stacked, you can be sure of some real smooth and enjoyable viewing.

Rearrange your apps

The moment you are done installing your apps, you could proceed with reordering your apps with the favorites on top. To reorder the list, hit the (*) button as you highlight any app, and choose "Move channel." You can implement the arrow or navigational keys for selecting a new position and hit on OK when you are through.

Hide (any) unwanted menu

Do you dislike Fandango's TV as well as movie stores filling your main screen? Visit Settings > Main screen > Movie store and TV store, then select "Hide'"
Explore the hidden Wi-Fi menu for optimizing your reception.

One way to know the strength of your Wi-Fi signal is by looking up your Network menu, although you are only going to find out if its status is good or if it isn't. You need to use a hidden menu if you are interested in getting detailed information regarding your RokuWi-FIsignal strength. In order to access this hidden menu, go to your home page. Press the home screen button that is on the remote for 5 times, and then up, down, up, down, up.

Doing that will display your Wi-Fi signal along with all the necessary information. Should your device indicate weak signal, moving the antenna of your router about can help to better the reception.

Discover free stuff

When it comes to free content, there is plenty of it from Roku. You can download free video applications like Pluto TV, Sony Crackle, Roku Channel and Tubi; however, you could equally follow up on free shows and movies via your Roku menu.

The Featured Free screen is for digging up free shows and movies from several apps, including those mentioned above. If you seek something particular – and you've got a Roku which works with voice control – you could search for particular genres with your voice. Just say "free science-fiction" or "free sitcoms" shows, and Roku will provide with a list of result, with at least one source being free.

Play content via your smartphone

Casting on your Roku is not restricted to apps such as Kodi and YouTube. You could equally play content that is stored in your smartphone via your TV by employing Roku' mobile app. Looking at the app' bottom menu, you will discover a Photos button. Choose the Photo menu, and you would come across a screen that will grant you access to videos, photos and music stored inside your smartphone. Well, you have to be careful with this feature though, particularly if you do not save your "personal" photos to a different folder within your smartphone.

Track what you are watching

Use the "My Feed" module of Roku home page to track specific shows, movies, directors or even actors and be instantly informed whenever anything new happens. Search for anything, and then look for "Follow on Roku" among the result. You could equally browse for shows and movies that you follow through "My Feed" section.

Watch secret private channels

Roku became many people' choice when it provided users with access to stream the most famous networks within the digital space, but that is not all. Roku lets user create their private channels for streaming content, which amounts to an entertaining niche of networks. Discover unusual horror, lost TV shows for children, and unavailable movies. You do not need to do anything special since we already have a ready-made list of all the best Roku secret channels to get you started.

Navigate faster

Assuming your Roku is now stuffed with content and apps, you could apply these tips for getting around with only few clicks via your remote:

On your home page, hit fast forward or rewind for paging up or down via your application list. This equally works in many menus as well as several third-party applications.
Return to the beginning of your application list from any screen by tapping the home screen button twice.

In some other apps, for example Netflix, you can press the play button even as you highlight a program for skipping the description page and streaming right away.

Using Your Replay button

Longed for a little dialog that was difficult to hear? Press the replay button on the remote (the button with the counter-clockwise symbol) to move 10 seconds backwards. You can equally set your replay button so that it includes captions by accessing Settings > Accessibility > Captions mode, and then select "On replay."

Set the streaming bits rate the way you want

Have you had to deal with the ordeal associated with data cap? You need some good amount of data to be able to stream HD video for hours non-stop; hence if you are streaming on low data, you could explore this hack to aid you in reducing the amount of used data. Roku users are privileged with a particular debug option that allows you to set the bit rate at which your contents streams with. activating this menu requires that you press the Home button 5 times, rewind 3 times, and eventually fast forward 2 times. That button combination activate the Roku override page. When you see that, you can set the limits based on what you can afford.

Make dialog simple to understand

Roku has some straightforward ways for normalizing the volume on streaming players. The Night mode reduces the volume in loud scenes, whereas Leveling is for compressing the entire volume range for hearing quiet scenes and not getting jolted by some other sound

Customize a screensaver (with Android only)

Are you feeling a bit bored with Roku' standard screensaver? Use photos of yourself instead with Roku free Android app. Launch the app, go to "Photos+" tab, and select screensaver, then choose the photos you would love to use. (Unfortunately, this feature is unavailable for RokuiOS app.) When you have added the photos, go to Settings > Screensaver > Change screensaver inside your Roku player, and select "Roku Mobile sreensaver."

Listening privately (with Bluetooth or wired headphones)

Should you have Roku Ultra or any player that has 3.5mm jack incorporated in the remote, you could listen privately as you plug in any ear buds or headphones.

For some other Roku player, listening privately can be done via Rokus free app for android and iOS. Go to the app's "Remote" tab, press the menu on top the screen, then toggle "Private Listening" to on. You can now plug in your wired headphones, use wireless earbuds, or listen via your phone speakers.

Send video from YouTube&Netflix

With YouTube and Netflix, you could have videos sent from a tablet or phone to Roku player, like you normally do with Google Chromecast streamer. With your Roku on a similar Wi-Fi network, open either YouTube or Netflix, press Cast button and select Roku from the outputted list. Any of the videos you select will be seen on your TV rather than your smartphone or tablet. This is also possible with a computer that works with Google Chrome browser.

if you enjoy beaming your private media contents to Roku, using AllCast is the best way to go about it. (The Roku can offer the same functionality, although the interface is not user-friendly and it does not work with cloud storages.) the moment you open the app, it detects your Roku right away, presenting you with options to select videos, photos as well as music that can be played on large screens. (Getting rid of ads as well as movie time limits would require the Premium app that costs $5)

Connect Your Google Assistant for a playback control

Roku can now work with Google Home speakers as well as other Google Assistant based devices, that lets you control playbacks and launch apps via voice command. On Roku' smart Televisions, the inputs and volume can equally be controlled by Google Assistants.

Setting this up requires that you launch the Google Home application, press "Add" on the main page. Choose "Set up device," and select "Works with Google." Select Roku from outputted list, log into your account, then select the Roku device you wish to connect. (Sadly, only one Roku can be linked with Google Assistant.) When it is connected, you could say stuffs like Hey Google, pause on Roku," or "Hey Google, open Amazon Prime on Roku."

Listening to music with great ease

Should your Roku include a voice remote – or maybe you are using the mobile app remote that functions with Roku supported devices – you could employ voice commands for launching music on Pandora directly, TuneIn and iHeartRadio. (TuneIn and HeartRadio equally support podcasts.) Press your remote' microphone button and utter something such as "listen to Thumbprint Radio on Pandora." or "listen to Jazz." You could equally ask for a particular recording artist. For deciding your default music service, you could go to the official Roku website.

Navigate through Roku channels on your smartphone

Roku devices come with one remote, but for a better experience the mobile app is most preferred. Roku's remote app can be found oniOs and Android, providing you with complete user control, on the condition that the smartphone is using that very Wi-Fi connection. Choose channels from the list that comes up on your smartphone, change subtitles, rewind. You would appreciate this if your kids are used to misplacing your remote.

Watch hidden private channels

Roku became many people' choice when it provided users with access to stream the most famous networks within the digital space, but that is not all. Roku lets user create their private channels for streaming content, which amounts to an entertaining niche of networks. Discover unusual horror, lost TV shows for children, and unavailable movies.

Conclusion

Once you start to implement the steps outlined you will be able to use your Roku device like a pro. Good luck and enjoy!